STRENGTH

GRATITUDE

Sara Antill

PowerKiDS press

New York

Published in 2014 by The Rosen Publishing Group, Inc.
29 East 21st Street, New York, NY 10010

First Edition

Editor: Jennifer Way
Book Design: Greg Tucker

Photo Credits: Cover, pp. 7, 11 Jupiterimages/Creatas/Thinkstock; p. 4 Transcendental Graphics/Getty Images; p. 5 Bruno Fahy/AFP/Getty Images; p. 6 Darrin Henry/ Shutterstock.com; pp. 9, 19 Monkey Business Images/Shutterstock.com; p. 10 New York Daily News Archive/Getty Images; p. 12 Otto Greule Jr./Getty Images; p. 13 Mike Coppola/WireImage/Getty Images; p. 14 Frederick Breedon/FilmMagic /Getty Images; p. 15 Paul Bradbury/OJO Images/Getty Images; p. 17 Barry Austin/Digital Vision/Getty Images; p. 18 iStockphoto/Thinkstock; p. 20 Steve Granitz/WireImage/Getty Images; p. 21 JupiterImages/Brand X Pictures/Thinkstock.

Library of Congress Cataloging-in-Publication Data

Antill, Sara.
  Gratitude / by Sara Antill. — 1st ed.
      p. cm. — (Character strength)
  Includes index.
  ISBN 978-1-4488-9681-3 (library binding) — ISBN 978-1-4488-9820-6 (pbk.) — ISBN 978-1-4488-9821-3 (6-pack)
  1. Gratitude. I. Title.
  BF575.G68A58 2013
  179'.9—dc23
                              2012029012
Manufactured in the United States of America

CPSIA Compliance Information: Batch #S13PK2: For Further Information contact Rosen Publishing, New York, New York at 1-800-237-9932

Contents

AN ATTITUDE OF GRATITUDE

In the United States, we celebrate Thanksgiving as a day of **gratitude**, or thankfulness. However, gratitude is an **attitude**, or outlook, that some people have all year. In fact, gratitude is just one character strength that many successful people share.

Lou Gehrig (1903-1941)

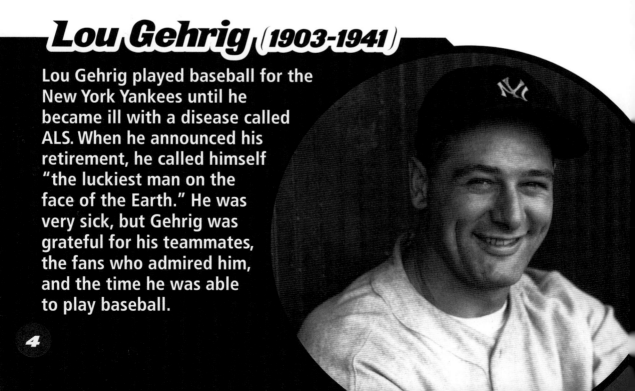

Lou Gehrig played baseball for the New York Yankees until he became ill with a disease called ALS. When he announced his retirement, he called himself "the luckiest man on the face of the Earth." He was very sick, but Gehrig was grateful for his teammates, the fans who admired him, and the time he was able to play baseball.

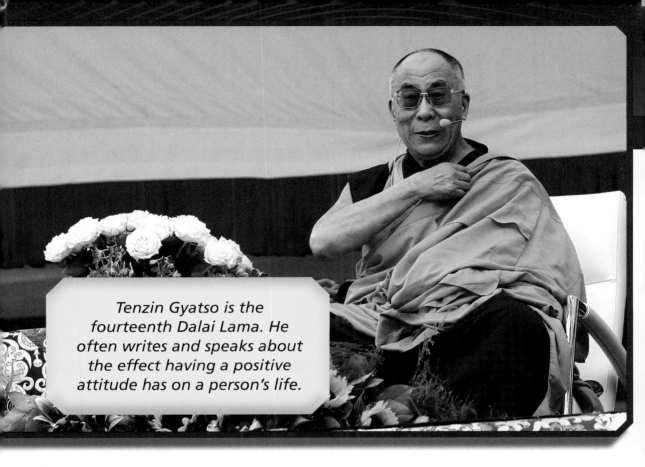

Tenzin Gyatso is the fourteenth Dalai Lama. He often writes and speaks about the effect having a positive attitude has on a person's life.

Tenzin Gyatso is the spiritual leader of Buddhism from the area of Tibet. He is often called by his title, the Dalai Lama. He lives his life with gratitude. He has said that each day when he wakes up, he is happy just to be alive. Do you wake up each day with gratitude? This book will help you find gratitude in yourself and others!

WHAT IS GRATITUDE?

People with gratitude are thankful for the good things that happen to them. They also understand that even when bad things happen to them, it can make them stronger people. Someone with gratitude **appreciates** other people and their strengths, too. Studies have shown that people's sense of gratitude grows as they mature.

A sense of gratitude helps you appreciate the value of learning. This might make you want to do your best in school.

Some adults who serve in the military do so out of a sense of gratitude to their country.

People with gratitude understand the value of things. Some kids wish they did not have to go to school every day. People with gratitude know the value of a good education. They are grateful to their teachers for their help and dedication. **Recognizing** value and good **opportunities** is a great step toward success!

HALF FULL OR HALF EMPTY?

Imagine a glass with water reaching the halfway line. Would you think that the glass is half full? Do you think it is half empty? We use the question of the half-full glass to ask whether someone is looking at either the positive or the **negative** side of things.

Looking at the positive side of things can make you more aware of the good things around you. A person with gratitude thinks more about the things he has instead of the things he does not have. Being aware of good things makes it easier to be grateful for them.

People with gratitude value having good friends. Our relationships with others help "fill the glass" more than toys or other things can.

GIVING BACK

An important part of living with gratitude is being thankful for the people around you. Start by looking at the ways your family helps one another. Author Studs Terkel wanted people to appreciate how all Americans contribute to their country. He collected the stories of ordinary people to show that everyone contributes something special to America.

Studs Terkel (1912-2008)

Studs Terkel was an author and oral historian. This is someone who interviews and gathers the stories of people's lives. He gathered people's stories about World War II, the Great Depression, and even stories about people's jobs. While others may have thought the people he talked to were not important, Terkel appreciated the value of their stories.

Another way to show gratitude is to volunteer in your community.

You can practice your gratitude by saying "thank you." You can also show your gratitude by helping others. You might offer to wash the vegetables for dinner to help your parents. You can even offer to do one of your brother's chores so he can study for a big test.

GRATITUDE ON THE BASEBALL FIELD

Derek Jeter is a very successful baseball player. He plays shortstop for the New York Yankees. When Derek was growing up, his father worked to help people who had problems with drugs and alcohol. In 1996, Derek started a **charity** called the Turn 2 Foundation. This group works to help kids turn away from drugs and alcohol and toward healthy lifestyles.

Derek Jeter's positive attitude means he is seen as a leader by his Yankee teammates. He has been the Yankees' captain since 2003.

Here is Derek Jeter with a group of schoolchildren at a Turn 2 holiday party.

Jeter lives his life with gratitude to his family, his teammates, and his **community**. His foundation is just one of the many ways that he has found to give back. Jeter's gratitude and positive attitude inspire his teammates and others!

LOOK ON THE BRIGHT SIDE

Gratitude is an inner **resource** that helps you push yourself toward success. People who take part in the Paralympics are athletes who were either born with disabilities or who became disabled through accidents or illnesses. They focus on pursuing the extraordinary athletic abilities they have rather than on their disabilities.

When bad things happen, many people get sad, angry, or frustrated. Living with gratitude helps you look on the bright side.

Carrie Underwood (1983-)

Carrie Underwood is a Grammy Award-winning country singer. The *American Idol* winner grew up on a farm in Checotah, Oklahoma. In 2009, Underwood started a foundation that helps her hometown. She said creating the foundation was important because she wanted to show gratitude to the community for the support it gave to her growing up.

Instead of seeing a move as sad or scary, think of it as a new adventure for you and your family!

Perhaps your parent gets a new job, and your family must move to a new town. Instead of being upset, focus on the positive. You can be grateful for the friends that you have and for the new ones that you will meet. You can be thankful for your parent's new job.

GRATITUDE ALL AROUND

On Thanksgiving, many families go around the dinner table and list the things they are grateful for. You may hear something listed and realize you are thankful for it, too. You do not have to wait until Thanksgiving to talk about gratitude, though. When people talk to each other about what they are grateful for, it is easier for everyone to appreciate the good things in their lives.

When you see someone living with gratitude, let him know that you like his good attitude. Learning to see gratitude in others will help you recognize your own gratitude, too!

You should feel proud when you reach a goal or win an award. Remember to show gratitude to the people who helped you and supported you, though!

MAKE A GRATITUDE LIST

Living with gratitude is easy when you are aware of the good things around you. When you wake up each morning, try to think of at least three things you are grateful for. As you go through the day, be on the lookout for even more things to be grateful for.

If you can think of 3 things you are thankful for, why not try to list 5, or even 10 things?

If you feel grateful for something special a family member has done for you, be sure to tell her. Everyone likes to feel appreciated by others.

Try making a gratitude list. Everyone has bad days sometimes. The next time you are having a bad day, though, look at your list. You will be reminded of the good things in your life and may even think of more to add!

A PERFECT BALANCE

Living with gratitude helps people recognize opportunities and become successful. For example, Senator Daniel Inouye lost his right arm fighting in World War II. His gratitude and grit helped him recover from this injury, and his zest motivated him to serve his country as a senator for over 50 years! It is important to **balance** your strengths.

Aron Ralston (1975-)

While rock climbing in 2003, Aron Ralston's right arm was pinned under a boulder. After being trapped for five days, he cut off his arm to get free. Instead of feeling sad about losing an arm, Ralston felt gratitude for surviving. The movie *127 Hours* was made about his ordeal.

Teamwork is a balance of strengths. It is important to have zest to boost your team's spirits. It is also important to show gratitude for your teammates' efforts.

Someone with zest might get so excited that she forgets to appreciate the work of others. Someone with a lot of gratitude, though, will credit others for the part they play. Balancing all your strengths will help you better use each one.

MY REPORT CARD: GRATITUDE

How much gratitude do you show each day? Using a separate sheet of paper, check off how many of the following statements about gratitude sound like you. Be honest! If you are not happy with your score, you can practice showing your gratitude for a while, and then test yourself again.

- ☐ I try to look for the positive side of a situation.
- ☐ I appreciate what other people do for me.
- ☐ I try to help others any way I can.
- ☐ When I say "thank you," I really mean it.
- ☐ I give others the credit they deserve.
- ☐ I know that I have many good opportunities in my life.
- ☐ I value my education.
- ☐ I often think about the things for which I am thankful.
- ☐ I try to give back and help my family, school, and community.
- ☐ I **encourage** others to live with gratitude.

Glossary

appreciates (uh-PREE-shee-ayts) Is thankful for something or someone.

attitude (A-tuh-tood) A person's outlook or position.

balance (BAL-ens) To have the right mix of things.

charity (CHER-uh-tee) A group that gives help to the needy.

community (kuh-MYOO-nih-tee) A place where people live and work together or the people who make up such a place.

credit (KREH-dit) The honor that someone who does something special gets.

encourage (in-KUR-ij) To give hope, cheer, or certainty.

gratitude (GRA-tuh-tood) Being thankful.

negative (NEH-guh-tiv) Looking at the bad side of things.

opportunities (ah-per-TOO-nih-tee) Good chances.

recognizing (REH-kig-nyz-ing) Knowing from past knowledge.

resource (REE-sawrs) A supply, source of energy, or other useful thing.

Index

Websites

Due to the changing nature of Internet links, PowerKids Press has developed an online list of websites related to the subject of this book. This site is updated regularly. Please use this link to access the list: www.powerkidslinks.com/char/grati/